A CiRCE Guide to

Reading

Andrea Lipinski & Andrew Kern

Published in the USA
by the CiRCE Institute
© 2017 CiRCE Institute

For information
CiRCE Institute
81 McCachern Blvd
Concord, NC 28025
www.circeinstitute.com

Cover design by Graeme Pitman.

Printed in the United States of America

The key to reading well is to treat books like people.

Don't try to introduce yourself to everybody; make some good friends and true.

Enjoy them, don't make them your servants.

Spend time with them because you want to.

Let them teach you whatever they know and thank them for it.

Don't wring truths out of them they don't want to tell you.

Don't demand everything in a moment and don't force them to be efficient.

Don't throw them away when they don't do things your way.

Enjoy them for what they draw out of you, reveal about you to yourself, and help you see in others.

Work on important projects together.

Go to school together if you have to, but save your best times for at home, under or up the tree, by the river, in the fields, on a walk, riding the bus, going for a drive, or wherever you most like to be.

Introduce them to other people you love.

Think about them when they aren't around.

Remember them fondly and even boast about their glories to others.

Let them change you because you love them.

Read them humbly and don't try too hard to tell them what they mean.

- Andrew Kern

Contents

Preface

Every story has a point or an idea that guides the author in each artistic decision he makes—what to include, how to arrange it, or how to express it. Sometimes he knows rather precisely what that idea is from the beginning, and on rare occasions he may even be able to express it in a single sentence—like the moral of a fable or the thesis of an essay. More often, it is the act of telling the story that helps him figure out its point. Or on some occasions he may tell a whole story and never figure out or comprehend the idea the story reveals. But there always is a point, whether it is easy to express or not!

Consider the story Nathan told David when he had to confront him for taking another man's wife and then ensuring the man would be killed in battle. Nathan did not tell a story about a man stealing another man's wife. Nor did Nathan tell a story about a man killing another man. Instead, he told King

David a story about two men, one rich and the other poor. The rich man had his own herds with many lambs, but the poor man had only one precious ewe lamb which was like a daughter to him. One day when the rich man welcomed a traveler, the rich man took the poor man's lamb to serve to the guest.

After Nathan told this story, King David was furious at the rich man. Then Nathan revealed that he, King David, was that rich man. The point he was trying to make guided Nathan each time he had a decision to make about what to include.

This is not as deep or odd an idea as it might seem at first. If you have ever begun to say something, paused, hesitated, reconsidered, maybe even said, "No, that's not it..." or, "Wait, let me think..." you have experienced in a sentence what a story-teller wrestles with throughout a whole story.

Ask yourself: When you say, "That's not what I wanted to say," how do you know? It seems evident that something precedes your words—a goal, a desired means of expression, an idea that was guiding you to choose the right words to form a sentence that would carry the idea from your own mind into the mind of another through the little sound-pictures we call words. If you were able to say what you meant and if the listener was able to understand, you communicated successfully.

Happily, all of us follow a similar pattern when we try to communicate. It's an amazingly flexible pattern, too, applying to every sentence anybody has ever spoken, and enabling friendships to grow, covenants and agreements to be settled, decisions to be made, and people and events to be remembered. The more skillfully we can use it, the more effectively we can take the ideas that flit around in our minds like ghosts and shadows and give them bodies with wings that can fly from mind to mind. The technical term for this pattern is Grammar and its virtue is that it enables us to effectively send ideas between our minds.

In the classical world, the Greeks had a word for this: the point or truth that the author or speaker tries to express in a sentence, a story, or a text (in fact, in any work of art). The word is *logos*, and it is the key to all understanding and art and wisdom. *Logos* is a word with vast meaning, including "word," "reason," or even "study." But the main notion seems to be that of a unifying principle, like the sun that holds together the solar system.

One of the benefits a logos offers an author or artist is that it serves as a principle to help him know what to include and where to include it. His goal is to embody that logos in every detail of his sentence or artifact (i.e. work of art).

When you hesitated over that sentence we talked about earlier, it was probably because you weren't confident that the words or phrases you were using effectively expressed your logos. But notice: The logos was there before you tried to express or embody it. Yet, you could not communicate it until you embodied it.

When the logos guides the artist, it holds the work of art (or sentence) together; it serves as a unifying or harmonizing principle. Imagine for a moment that right now I started to write about whether Joe Montana or Tom Brady is better. It would break the unity of this little essay. It would not cohere, and would demonstrate that I have forgotten my logos. What makes a good writer a good writer is the ability to express his logos in every detail of his writing without losing it at any point. Every detail reveals the logos a little more.

What on earth does all this have to do with reading?

Simply this: Reading and writing are acts of communication, analogous to listening and speaking. If the goal of writing is to express a logos, the goal of reading is to perceive it. If we forget this, we will approach reading in ways that produce unskilled readers, thinkers, communicators, and decision-makers.

This reading guide provides teachers and readers with tools that equip readers to think about, play with, wrestle with, maybe even do battle with, a text. It begins with the recognition that reading is an act of communication—of listening—in which the most important thing is to receive the logos that has been communicated by the writer.

In particular, story-telling is a sort of game that the story-teller plays with the reader or listener. The reader gets better by playing and by watching others play who are better at it.

The reader's goal is to grasp the writer's logos. There are rules that govern the way the game is played and techniques and skills that help the reader succeed. If the reader "wins," he finds that the joy of it is, in a way, similar to figuring out a math problem or laughing at a joke: "I got it!" he says.

Got what? The logos—the idea—the point!

This guide helps the reader play the game and master the skills that enable him to perceive the logos—in short to become a master reader. Its ultimate goal is not to help students perform better on homework and test-taking (though it will be remarkably helpful even for these purposes), but to help him experi-

ence the deep pleasures, riches, and comforts to be found in
literature and to grow in wisdom and virtue.

Introduction

You hold in your hands a guide to reading that is drawn from experience supplemented by the literature on reading and suggestions gathered over years of teaching and discussing books. If you are acquainted with books on reading, you may recognize tools and approaches like SQ3R, speed reading, normative reading, inspectional reading, etc.

However, this guide is not driven by techniques, but by purpose: Its goal is to enable readers to better participate in a dialogue with a written text, and the purpose of that dialogue is communication. Therefore, techniques are useful when they help the reader better listen and respond to the writer.

The approach we take is drawn from the nature of reading which is complex, like any conversation. But underlying the complexity, there are questions common to every reader about any text. When readers learn to answer these common questions, the more particular questions about a given text or specific to a reader become much easier to answer.

When goals are appropriate, sound techniques, methods, and tools follow. This guide shows you skills and tools such as layered reading, highlighting in multiple colors, and margin notes. As a flexible system, it will help any reader read more closely and attentively. Mastery of these tools both increases the reader's pleasure and fortifies his study skills.

The guide is written in a way that enables you to use it by yourself or to lead a discussion about it. Each chapter is divided into six sections that teach you a tool, reveal its purpose, and allow you to practice using it.

These sections are:

Contemplate: Prepare for the lessson by reflecting on questions related to the logos of the lesson.

Consider: Analogies and examples of the logos.

Compare: Questions that help you compare the examples and analogies with each other.

Describe: You describe how to do what you have learned in that lesson.

Practice: An activity to put what you learned into action.

Stretch: An activity to excercise what you've learned in a book of your choice.

Why layered reading?

Katerina Kern once prepared a class of sophomores to learn the tools in this book. She engaged her students in a simple process to prepare them for what followed. First, she instructed a student to read aloud a page from a class text. Then she asked him to close the book and asked the class what they remembered. Students restated some names and places, while they wondered when the events of the book occurred. She wrote these notes on the board.

Then she asked a volunteer to read the same passage aloud again. After instructing the reader to close the book, she asked her students what they could recall this time. They mentioned actions performed by characters, sometimes in an orderly sequence and sometimes not. Students began to wonder both why the actions were performed and what would result.

For the third time, Katerina asked a volunteer to read the same page aloud. Afterward, she asked them again to tell her what they recalled. This time they recalled more details, made causal connections, and answered their own questions.

Then she repeated the same three steps with a second text and had similar results.

Afterward, Katerina asked her students to compare what they remembered after the first reading and discussed what sorts of things tended to come up. They restated mostly proper nouns, names, and places. They also noticed (and were bothered) that they couldn't remember when the events were taking place.

Next, she asked them to look at the items they recalled after the second time they read the text and to express what those items have in common. After a second read, the students noticed the actions of the characters.

Finally, she asked them to compare what they recalled after the third reading. Students noticed ideas, made comparisons, and answered their own questions.

This exercise helped her students realize that the human mind asks questions in layers. It tends to seek a certain kind of information first, another kind second, and yet another third. The first layer of information is "who," "where," and "when." Next, the mind seeks to know what the "who" is doing (at that time, in that place). The third layer the mind attends to is how things compare, how they are related, what is most important, and other more abstract questions.

I (Andrea) tried the same exercise with a seventh grader and had a similar experience. And when I tried it again with a group of teachers, the same pattern played out. I concluded that the best way to read is in layers so our minds can seek answers in the pattern that seems most natural.

Because the higher level questions depend on the lower, readers find it most effective to answer the lower or more basic questions first. Happily, with a little practice they can often do it in a matter of seconds, as you will see in Part One, scanning. Then in Part Two, reading, you will see how the foundations laid in part one lead to much closer, more insightful reading. Following that, in part three, you will learn ways to hold on to what you have learned, absorb it, and share it with others.

To prepare yourself and your students to read attentively, actively, and purposefully, guide your students through Katerina's lesson described above.

Read Aloud and Respond

1. Depending on their ability to think abstractly, ask

your students, "What does your mind do when you read? What do you need to know to be able to read?" Discuss what they suggest.

2. Read aloud a short, unfamiliar passage, above the students' independent reading level. For example, read a paragraph or two from the beginning of a chapter in Plutarch's *Lives* or a Jane Austen novel.

3. Ask the students what they recall. Write this on a board.

4. Read aloud the same passage again.

5. Ask the students to share what they remember. Write this on the board in a separate group.

6. Read aloud the same passage for the final time.

7. Ask the students what they recall. Write this on the board in a separate group.

Repeat

Repeat the above sequence with a second passage.

Compare

1. Ask the students how the responses after the first reading were similar and different.

2. Ask the students how the responses after the second reading were similar and different.

3. Ask the students how the responses after the third reading were similar and different.

Describe

Ask your students to describe the sorts of thing they remember after each reading. Do you see the same sort of pattern that Katerina and Andrea saw? Most groups will, but if they don't, don't dwell on it. Just help them understand that they look for information in layers and that they remember some things because their minds were asking for that information.

Reading is a question-driven dialogue and those questions are asked in more or less the same order each time.

Practice

By strengthening your reading skills through the exercises and tools taught in this guide, you develop your imagination and attend to what David Hicks calls normative ends in *Norms and Nobility*: the contemplation of truth, goodness, and beauty. Continue to Part One to learn about scanning in more detail.

Nota Bene

The tools you learn in this Reading Guide are meant to assist you, not to be your master. As you master them you will decide when to use them and how. At first, you will almost certainly use them badly, because that is how we learn anything. Your skills will improve with practice. But always remember, the tools are for you to use for your own purposes.

Part One
Scanning

Chapter One
A Question-guided Dialogue

....

"You have been given questions to which you cannot be given answers. You will have to live them out— perhaps a little at a time."

Wendell Berry,
Jayber Crow

Before you read a book closely, you will scan it a few times. Like preparing the soil, this can seem distracting or pointless, but how well you perform these actions will profoundly impact how well you read.

Contemplate

- Why do you read books?
- What is order? What is harmony?
- How many questions can you answer at one time?

Consider

Early one evening a family prepared their dinner and discussed the day. The children moved in and out of the kitchen as well as in and out of the discussion. Suddenly the children rushed up to their father and bombarded him with questions. Overwhelmed, he stopped them by holding up his index finger and saying, "one at a time. You are first." The children relaxed as he patiently gave his attention to each child in turn.

When we read, a number of questions crowd our minds, demanding our attention like the children in the anecdote. Our minds want to know super practical things, like, "How long is this book? How long will it take to read it?" Plot elements like, "Who is the hero? When does it take place? Where does it take place" Genre questions, like, "Is it a mystery? A history? A fantasy?" Moral questions like, "Will the characters do anything foolish? Should I root for the hero? Who are the good guys?" And even very personal questions, like, "Do I like this writer? Would my sister like this book?"

We cannot answer these questions at the same time, yet they all crowd around, waiting for an answer. Over the years, we learn to ignore them, but that only makes them a little sulkier and more unhelpful. But if we would answer them, they would help us read better.

Like the children who confidently knew the dad would answer each question, so our mind needs to know that its questions will be respected and answered. When they know that they will be answered in time, they are able to relax and wait their turns.

Like the father who stopped the children and let them ask their questions one at a time, so a skillful and wise reader attends to the questions in his head in an orderly way.

Happily, most of these questions are easy enough to answer and only take a few seconds. Furthermore, most of them are common questions that every reader asks, though some may not realize it.

To help the reader respond in an orderly way, this guide teaches "layered reading." It introduces three broad stages to reading: scanning, reading, and reviewing. Part One demonstrates scanning. Part Two explains reading. And Part Three introduces skills useful for review. Scanning involves multiple layers, reading proper is laid on top of the scanning layers, and then review looks back at the whole image constructed through the layers.

Layered reading offers a way of preparing your mind to become acquainted with a particular book.

Compare

- How is answering the questions asked by a roomful of children like reading a book? How is it different?

- How is scanning different from reading proper? How is reading in layers like any other activity that involves multiple steps? How is it different? Choose any activity with which you are familiar.
- How is layered reading different from a single read?

Describe

Describe layered reading in your own words.

Practice

Continue to Chapter Two on scanning to implement what you have learned in this chapter.

Stretch

Choose another book that you will read while you complete this reading guide. Keep it nearby for future exercises. We will refer to this book from now on as your "companion book."

You may choose your companion book for many reasons: a teacher assigned it for a class, you assigned the book for a class, you have already read the whole book once, or you just purchased a new book. If possible, try to complete the "stretch" exercise in each chapter with a book you have already read once. Use a book that is challenging but not so difficult as to discourage you. C. S. Lewis' *Abolition of Man*, The Chronicles of Narnia Series, and *Hannah Coulter* by Wendell Berry are good places to begin, depending on your previous reading.

<u>Nota Bene</u>

Be sure to read and practice the Intro-duction. Try the exercise on your unsus-pecting spouse, friend, or students. Teach-ers must establish in students the need for these reading skills, and the skills will cre-ate the affection for a book. The Introduc-tion explains the steps to create this need, or awareness, in students. The remaining chapters present the scanning, reading, and reviewing skills.

Notes

Chapter Two
Initial Scan

"For which of you, desiring to build a tower, does not first sit down and count the cost, whether he has enough to complete it? Otherwise, when he has laid a foundation and is not able to finish, all who see it begin to mock him, saying, 'This man began to build and was not able to finish.'"

Luke 14: 28-30

The initial scan is unusual because you aren't yet looking for anything in particular. You are just getting the lay of the land, so to speak; seeing what is there in only the most general sense.

Strictly speaking, you aren't scanning (which involves looking for specific things, the way a radar looks for an airplane) but skimming (which only notes what you discover on the surface, the way a skimmer removes the fat globules from milk).

Also, while this chapter goes into some detail about the sorts of things you might notice and therefore takes a few minutes to read and practice, your actual initial scan, or skim, takes only a few seconds. But don't skip it!

Let's learn how to skim.

Contemplate

- Imagine you have just arrived at a new location where you might want to build a house. What would your eyes do in the first few seconds? What are you likely to notice?
- What if you wanted to picnic there?
- Or play a game?
- Imagine that a general arrives at a potential battlefield before both his armies and the enemy. What is he likely to notice in the first few seconds?
- If you pick up a book for the first time, what are some of the first things you notice?

Consider

After we (Andrea's family) decided to build a tree house, our project planning was initiated by a few very general questions which we quickly answered: What were the features of the terrain? How did the sun shine on it? What kind of wood was available? In the back of our minds were the questions: Is it even possible? How much will it cost? How long will it take?

When we decide to read a book, our minds want to know similar information, especially, perhaps, how much time it will take. This is a good question because we all have limited time and nobody can read every book he wants to. We also want to know things like how many pages it has, how the sections are divided, how hard the font is to read, how it is laid out, whether it includes charts, and many other easily identified details.

To answer these questions and many more, scan the book quickly, gathering a few pieces of information to estimate how long it will take to read and to get a basic feel for the whole text (i.e. the features of the terrain).

Scanning is not reading: When you conduct the initial scan (the skim), you move your eyes quickly across pages or sections and notice whatever you see.

To begin an initial scan, flip through a book and notice a few things. At first, it might help to ask a few questions. For example:

- What do you see inside the cover?
- Does the book include a table of contents, an index, or an appendix?
- Is there a preface or a prologue?
- What about the font size and the margins?
- Do the margins have enough room for writing notes?
- Is the tale captured in prose, poetry, or pictures?
- How many pages are in the book and how long is each chapter?

If you are an experienced reader, you probably ask most of these questions without even pausing to notice yourself doing it.

When you ask them, it is a little like finding out someone is moving into the neighborhood; you don't know much about them yet, but they might become friends, so you ask very general questions.

Compare

- What do building a tree house, meeting a new person, arriving at a new place for a picnic or a game, and first picking up a book have in common?
- How are they different?
- How is skimming a book or text like reading it? How is skimming different from reading?
- How is skimming a magazine article or a blog post similar to skimming a novel? How is it different?

Describe

- Describe scanning with initial questions (skimming) in your own words.
- Explain how to skim something you intend to read.

Practice

1. Skim this Reading Guide. First, flip to the front and notice the first few pages. Does the book have a table of contents, preface, or prologue? What else do you notice (remember, only a brief glance!)?

2. Flip through the pages in the middle and notice the text.

What do you see? Are there paragraphs of prose, lines of poetry, or pictures with charts? What about the font? Is there much white space in the margins?

3. Flip to the back and notice any added sections. Is there an appendix, index, or notes? How many pages are in the book?

4. Flip through a specific section you might read, the next chapter for example. How many pages are in that chapter? How long do you think it will take you to read that chapter? Do you have that much time to read it now? What else do you notice? Anything unusual?

Scanning with Initial Questions

1. What do you notice?
2. Is there a table of contents?
3. Does the text include prose, poetry, or charts?
4. Describe the font in very general terms (size, clarity, darkness)
5. How much white space is there?
6. Is there an appendix, index, or notes?
7. How many pages does the book have?
8. How long is the chapter you are looking at?
9. How long will it take you to read?
10. What else do you notice? Anything unique or unusual?

Stretch

1. Pick up your companion book (the book you chose at the end of Chapter One).

2. Skim it, asking the same initial questions.

3. Notice how long it takes you to skim. It should not have taken very long.

4. Do you have the time to read this book? If the book is not assigned reading, does it seem worth reading? Are you ready to decide? If so, keep it nearby for future exercises. If not, choose another book and complete the same initial scan until you choose a book you judge worth reading that you can use for practice with this guide.

Nota Bene

After completing an initial scan, you may decide not to read a book. If a book does not answer your questions or if it will cost more time than you have, it is fitting to choose not to read it now. Sometimes we read books because a teacher assigns them. The assignment creates the questions. Yet, the reading is still your choice. After all, not all students choose to complete their reading. Remember: While reading this handbook, don't become a slave to the technique; start looking for Truth. Whichever book you choose to read, read it for the best reasons.

Notes

Chapter Three
Quick Scans

....

"For what you see and hear depends a good deal on where you are standing: it also depends on what sort of person you are."

C.S. Lewis
The Magician's Nephew

Contemplate

- Before he throws the football, what does a quarterback do with his eyes? How long does he have to do it? How much time does he take to think about what to do?
- When approaching to spike a volleyball, how long does a volleyball player scan for a hole? Is looking for a hole on the court helpful or necessary?
- Go back to the lot or the battlefield that you skimmed in the previous chapter. If you decide to stay and wander around, what sorts of things would you look for next?

Consider

Do you remember the tree fort Andrea's family was thinking about in the last chapter? They did their initial scan and noted a few things about the terrain. Having decided to continue the project, a new level of questions arose. Now they had to scan a little more closely. New questions might include the following: Where will the fort be built? Among three separated trees or amid a grove of many trees? How high will the platform be? How large will the whole tree house be? Will it be a place where a few friends can rappel or a place where just one person can read? Asking these second level questions enabled us to gather information that prepared us to complete the task.

In a similar way, a second reading scan asks questions that are a little more specific than the initial scan. This second level scan actually involves two quick scans: a straight scan and an "S" scan. A quick scan is painless and fast. It is much like an athlete scanning the soccer field for an open teammate or a mother scanning a laundry pile to see how many loads it will take to finish the job.

First, identify the chapter or section you will read. Next, place your relaxed flat hand near the top of the first page with the finger tips just below the top lines. Move your hand and eyes straight down the page at a rate of one to two seconds per page. Continue this straight scan down each page of the chapter. The reason you use your hand is to guide your eye, which does not naturally move this way. Be sure your *eyes* move over the words on the page and not your fingers. However, do not read the words. Force your eyes to move at the steady rate of one or two seconds per page until you complete the section.

Then, return to the first page of the section and place your relaxed flat hand near the top left corner of the page just under the top lines. Move your hand across the page in an S pattern, sweeping your hand from left to right, moving down a few lines, and moving right to left, continuing a curvy pattern down the page. You should sweep to each side no more than two times per page. Spend approximately two to four seconds on each page.

You are still not reading, though you are preparing to read in a much more perceptive way. This is because these quick scans prepare you for the next layer of information by pouring a great deal more into your subconscious mind than most of us realize. With very little effort, you are filling your mind with cues that make reading a great deal easier and more perceptive.

While quick scanning, you may notice particular words. This is fine. Relax your hand, eyes, and mind, knowing that you do not need to remember the words. Try not to pronounce them in your head, but don't worry too much about this either. If you force your eyes to keep moving forward, you won't have time to sub-vocalize.

Compare

- How is preparing to read a book like settling on a plot of land for a house, a picnic, a game, or a battle?
- How is a quick scan like skimming or scanning for initial information?
- How are the two quick scans like each other? How are they different?
- How does scanning change the way you read?

Describe

Describe a straight scan and an S scan in your own words.

Straight Scan and S Scan

1. Scan eyes and fingers straight down the page (one to two seconds per page).
2. What do you notice? Introductions or summaries? New terms? Questions within the text from the author? Maps, text boxes, or charts? Anything new?
3. Scan eyes and fingers down the page in an S shape (four seconds per page).
4. Do you notice anything new? For example, do you notice any words that seem to appear frequently?

Practice

1. Flip to the next chapter of this book.

2. Do a straight scan. Place your relaxed hand near the top of the page. Move your hand and eyes down the page at approximately one to two seconds per page. Continue down each page of the chapter. Stop at the end of that chapter.

3. Do an S scan. Return your relaxed hand to the top left corner of the first page. Move your hand in a sweeping motion from left to right, then down a few lines, and return to the left again. Repeat moving down a few lines and then sweep right again at approximately two to four seconds per page. Continue down the entire page in a sweeping S pattern and continue S scanning each page till you reach the end of the chapter.

Note: It is not necessary for you to make a list of things that you notice. That question is only included in this exercise so you can realize how many things you do notice when you scan. Most people find they notice more and more as they practice.

Stretch

1. Pick up your companion book.

2. Complete the straight and S scans for the next chapter in that book.

3. Notice how long it takes you to complete the quick scans. You or your students might find it helpful if somebody keeps a

rhythm and taps the desk for each scan when it is time to turn to the next page. Do this only as needed to get in the habit of moving quickly, which you might find hard to get used to.

4. Keep your companion book nearby for future exercises.

Notes

Chapter Four
Pink Scan

··

*"A man can do worse than be poor. He can miss alto-
gether the sight of the greatness of small things."*

Robert Farrar Capon
The Supper of the Lamb

Having taken about a minute to quick scan the chosen chapter or section, your mind has stored away quite a bit of information. Its questions are becoming more specific. The next one is something like this: Are there unfamiliar words? Who are the characters? Where does it happen? When?

To answer these questions, you complete a pink scan in which you highlight names, dates, places, and important or new words with a pink highlighter. You could call this a "reference scan" because it would be easy to build a glossary or key word list from it.

Contemplate

- When you meet a person for the first time, what are the first one or two questions you ask?
- When you read, what are some of the first obstacles to continuing or enjoying the text?
- What is a noun? What is a proper noun?
- What is different about the first letter in the name of a proper noun?
- How are dates represented in print?
- What do you do when you come across unfamiliar words?

Consider

One of the most frustrating and discouraging experiences for the mind is to come across unfamiliar words or situations without any strategy to deal with them. People choose from among a few options when this happens while they are reading. Sometimes we just ignore the words and hope it won't matter. Sometimes we stop and look them up. But a pink scan offers a third option: Discover and note them before you even read, so you have time to determine the best next step.

Do you remember completing the introduction activity, when you asked your students what they remembered after each reading? What sorts of thing did they remember after the first reading?

Generally speaking, what people remember consists of a few names, maybe a setting, an action or two, and when it happened. These are the things we remember because they are the things our minds look for. They help us feel like we know where we are in the text. To give the mind the information it seeks, we follow the quick scans with a pink scan.

Suppose you hear a tale of two brothers. These two brothers wanted to begin a new city, but they disagreed over where to build it. One brother decided to build a wall around his chosen location while the other brother mocked him. The cantankerous brother jumped over the wall to taunt his kin, but the building brother murdered his jesting brother and named the new city after himself.

Puzzled? What if I told you this murder took place on April 21, 753 BC in Rome. Now do you know the brothers? Romulus founded Rome after a quarrel with Remus in 753 BC.

We find it much easier to remember stories when we can identify the names, dates, and places that make them up. This is because stories happen to people while they are in particular places at specific times.

Of course, not everything we read is character focused. If I read a technical document or an expository essay, I am likely to find technical or abstract terms. Highlight in pink the ones that seem important. Sometimes technical terms are italicized or put in bold.

Even with a story, we sometimes do not notice an important term when we S scan. In that case, you can highlight it in pink when you notice it while reading. For terms that are harder to find, it is even more helpful to highlight them once you discover them.

To complete a pink scan, you scan the section you are preparing to read with a pink highlighter in hand. When you encounter a name, date, place, or word that seems important, you highlight it in pink. In particular, look for proper nouns. Capital letters and numerals often help; they are signposts.

Do not backtrack when you highlight. The highlighter must move from left to right and top to bottom, and so must your eyes. If you miss anything you can highlight it later.

You are still not reading, though your mind will be noticing a great deal more than it did during the earlier scans. Having quick scanned, your mind has already begun to notice quite a bit (probably more than you realize). And yet, you have only spent a few seconds on each page. You are almost ready to read it!

Pink highlighting helps us build our vocabulary, find ideas or characters when we return to the text and understand or even feel the sort of document we are reading. Highlighting important words before reading is like meeting people for the first time, learning their names, and shaking hands. It helps orient you to the text.

Compare

- How are characters in a story like key ideas in an essay or technical document?
- What role do proper nouns have in stories?
- How is a pink scan like the quick scans?
- How is it different?
- How does scanning in pink affect what you notice when you read?
- What kinds of "pinks" would you expect to find in, for example, history, myth, math, and Twitter? How are they likely to be the same, and how different?

Describe

Describe what and how to highlight in pink in your own words.

Scanning with Pink

1. Look for names, dates, places, and terms that seem important.
2. Highlight these words in pink.

Practice

1. Complete an initial scan of the paragraphs below.
2. Complete your quick scan (straight scan and S scan).
3. Complete your pink scan.

Practice

1. Complete an initial scan of the paragraphs below.

2. Complete your quick scan (straight scan and S scan).

3. Complete your pink scan.

"The Fisherman and the Fish" from *The Complete Works of Count Tolstoy*

A Fisherman caught a Fish. Said the Fish:

"Fisherman, let me go into the water; you see I am small: you will have little profit of me. If you let me go, I shall grow up, and then you will catch me when it will be worth while."

But the Fisherman said:

"A fool would be he who should wait for greater profit, and let the lesser slip out of his hands."

Bulfinch's *Mythology*: The Age of Fable, Chapter VI

"Bacchus, on a certain occasion, found his old school master and foster father, Silenus, missing. The old man had been drinking, and in that state had wandered away, and was found by some peasants, who carried him to their king, Midas. Midas recognized him, and treated him hospitably, entertaining him for ten days and nights with an unceasing round of jollity. On the eleventh day he brought Silenus back, and restored him in safety to his pupil. Whereupon Bacchus offered Midas his choice of whatever reward he might

wish. *He asked that whatever he might touch should be changed into GOLD. Bacchus consented, though sorry that he had not made a better choice. Midas went his way, rejoicing in his newly acquired power, which he hastened to put to the test. He could scarce believe his eyes when he found that a twig of an oak, which he plucked from the branch, became gold in his hand. He took up a stone and it changed to gold. He touched a sod and it did the same. He took an apple from the tree and you would have thought he had robbed the garden of the Hesperides. His joy knew no bounds, and as soon as he got home, he ordered the servants to set a splendid repast on the table. Then he found to his dismay that whether he touched bread, it hardened in his hand; or put a morsel to his lips, it defied his teeth. He took a glass of wine, but it flowed down his throat like melted gold."*

"In consternation at the unprecedented affliction, he strove to divest himself of his power; he hated the gift he had lately coveted. But all in vain; starvation seemed to await him. He raised his arms, all shining with gold, in prayer to Bacchus, begging to be delivered from his glittering destruction. Bacchus, merciful deity, heard and consented. 'Go,' said he, "to the river Pactolus, trace the stream to its fountain-head, there plunge in your head and body and wash away your fault and its punishment." He did so, and scarce had he touched the waters before the gold-creating power passed into them, and the river sands became changed into GOLD, as they remain to this day."

Plutarch's *Lives*, Volume I

"The pedigree of Alkibiades is said to begin with Eurysakes the son of Ajax, while on the mother's side he descended from Alkmaeon, being the son of Deinomache, the daughter of Megakles. His father

Kleinias fought bravely at Artemisium in a trireme fitted out at his own expense, and subsequently fell fighting the Boeotians, in the battle of Koronea. Alkibiades after this was entrusted to Perikles and Ariphron, the two sons of Xanthippus, who acted as his guardians because they were the next of kin. It has been well remarked that the friendship of Sokrates for him did not a little to increase his fame, seeing that Nikias, Demosthenes, Lamakus, Phormio, Thrasybulus, and Theramenes, were all men of mark in his lifetime, and yet we do not know the name of the mother of any one of them, while we know the name even of the nurse of Alkibiades, who was a Laconian, named Amykla, and that of Zopyrus, his paedagogus, one of which pieces of information we owe to Antisthenes, and the other to Plato. As to the beauty of Alkibiades, it is not necessary to say anything except that it was equally fascinating when he was a boy, a youth, and a man. The saying of Euripides, that all beauties have a beautiful autumn of their charms, is not universally true, but it was so in the case of Alkibiades and of a few other persons because of the symmetry and vigour of their frames. Even his lisp is said to have added a charm to his speech, and to have made his talk more persuasive. His lisp is mentioned by Aristophanes in the verses in which he satirises Theorus, in which Alkibiades calls him Theolus, for he pronounced the letter r like l. Archippus also gives a sneering account of the son of Alkibiades, who, he said, swaggered in his walk, trailing his cloak, that he might look as like his father as possible, and bends his affected neck, and lisping speaks."

Stretch

1. Return to your companion book.

2. Scan in pink the section you have selected to read.

3. Notice how long it takes to highlight in pink. While it will take a little longer than the quick scans, it should still take not more than a few seconds per page.

4. Keep your companion book nearby for the next exercise.

Notes

Chapter Five
Green Scan

It is very easy for a reader to feel lost in a text, so the thoughtful writer works hard to help him know where he is. If unknown words create one frustration for readers, another is created when the reader is trying to find his path through a text while he is "walking" on it.

Another way to look at it is to say that every text has a structure or pattern and the sooner you can identify that pattern, the more easily you will be able to follow the story or the argument.

The green highlighter helps you identify that structure or locate you on the path. As a result, you can read like Niggle, with "no sense of rush... quieter inside."

Contemplate

- Would it matter if the instructions for assembling a bicycle were arranged in a different order?
- What would happen to a body if you removed the skeleton? What if you put a mouse's skeleton in the body of an elephant?
- Does the shape of a building sometimes tell you what happens inside?
- Why do travelers use maps?
- What is an ordinal number? List some.
- What is a conjunctive adverb? List some.

Consider

Public speakers are often told to "tell the audience what you are going to say, say it, and tell them what you said." That's good advice because people like to know where they stand. Not knowing where you are on a journey is frustrating, so good writers (who are guiding our thoughts) give frequent reminders to the pilgrim reader to indicate what is coming next, what just happened, and so on. They use numbers, questions, summaries, lists, changes of setting, and even imperatives, all so the reader can follow what would otherwise be too confusing.

You have one scan left before you read your text, and it is one of the most helpful. The green scan identifies and highlights the cues the author gives to tell the reader what just happened and what is coming.

Since there are many different kinds of text, you do not want or need to memorize a prescribed set of rules. Rather, look for ways the author locates you: "What clues does the author give to signify what will happen next? What just happened? What is happening?"

For example, numbers can be structural clues. Some writers include Roman numerals at the beginning of sections. In plays, act and scene headings provide structural cues. Sometimes ordinal numbers (first, second, third) are included, other times adverbs like secondly, next, and last.

Conjunctive adverbs (e.g., however, moreover, subsequently) indicate relationships like cause and effect, sequence, or consequents.

Authors also use questions, imperatives, and summaries to cue the reader. When an author includes a question, the answer typically follows. Imperatives to a reader are also clues for what is coming next. If an author writes, "Now let us discover whether...," then the discovery should eventually follow. A summary statement alerts the reader to the focus of previous sentences. All of these structural words are present to help us weave our reading and our understanding together.

Expository and technical writing tend to include explicit cues. However, in narrative, they are often not as obvious. Narrative is commonly ordered much like a play: by settings. Watch when the setting changes, when characters come and go, and when dialogue begins or ends, particularly speeches. At first, you might need to scan more slowly to get the hang of this, but practice will help you go faster in time.

By recognizing structure and order, we come to perceive the relationships between things and we realize that the life of the book is embodied in its structure. We come to appreciate order. But we don't make it the end of our observations. Structure is a foundation, a skeleton, and never the spirit. But in this world at least, the spirit needs to accept the limits of a skeleton to make itself known.

Compare

- How is green highlighting like pink?
- How is it different?
- How does highlighting in green affect your reading?
- What does it cause you to notice that you might not have noticed without it?
- How can these experiences differ from one another?

Describe

Describe how to scan in green in your own words.

Scanning with Green

1. Scan left to right and from top to bottom, searching for cues about the structure: what is coming, what just happened, what is happening now?

2. Highlight each cue with green.

Practice

1. Complete an initial scan of the paragraphs below.

2. Complete your finger scan (straight scan and S scan).

3. Complete your pink scan.

4. Complete your green scan.

The Sidereal Messenger **by Galileo Galilei**

"Hitherto I have spoken of the observations which I have made concerning the Moon's body; now I will briefly announce the phenomena which have been, as yet, seen by me with reference to the Fixed Stars. And first of all the following fact is worthy of consideration: The stars, fixed as well as erratic, when seen with a telescope, by no means appear to be increased in magnitude in the same proportion as other objects, and the Moon herself, gain increase of size; but in the case of the stars such increase appears much less,

so that you may consider that a telescope, which (for the sake of illustration) is powerful enough to magnify other objects a hundred times, will scarcely render the stars magnified four or five times. But the reason of this is as follows: When stars are viewed with our natural eyesight they do not present themselves to us of their bare, real size, but beaming with a certain vividness, and fringed with sparkling rays, especially when the night is far advanced; and from this circumstance they appear much larger than they would if they were stripped of those adventitious fringes, for the angle which they subtend at the eye is determined not by the primary disc of the star, but by the brightness which so widely surrounds it. Perhaps you will understand this most clearly from the well-known circumstance that when stars rise just at sunset, in the beginning of twilight, they appear very small, although they may be stars of the first magnitude; and even the planet Venus itself, on any occasion when it may present itself to view in broad daylight, is so small to see that it scarcely seems to equal a star of the last magnitude. It is different in the case of other objects, and even of the Moon, which, whether viewed in the light of midday or in the depth of night, always appears of the same size. We conclude therefore that the stars are seen at midnight in uncurtailed glory, but their fringes are of such a nature that the daylight can cut them off, and not only daylight, but any slight cloud which may be interposed between a star and the eye of the observer. A dark veil or coloured glass has the same effect, for, upon placing them before the eye between it and the stars, all the blaze that surrounds them leaves them at once. A telescope also accomplishes the same result, for it removes from the stars their adventitious and accidental splendours before it enlarges their true discs (if indeed they are of that shape), and so they seem less magnified than other objects, for a star of the fifth or sixth magnitude seen through a telescope is shown as of the first magnitude only."

Aristotle's *Poetics*, translated by S. H. Butcher

"Poetry in general seems to have sprung from two causes, each of them lying deep in our nature. First, the instinct of imitation is implanted in man from childhood, one difference between him and other animals being that he is the most imitative of living creatures, and through imitation learns his earliest lessons; and no less universal is the pleasure felt in things imitated. We have evidence of this in the facts of experience. Objects which in themselves we view with pain, we delight to contemplate when reproduced with minute fidelity: such as the forms of the most ignoble animals and of dead bodies. The cause of this again is, that to learn gives the liveliest pleasure, not only to philosophers but to men in general; whose capacity, however, of learning is more limited. Thus the reason why men enjoy seeing a likeness is, that in contemplating it they find themselves learning or inferring, and saying perhaps, 'Ah, that is he.' For if you happen not to have seen the original, the pleasure will be due not to the imitation as such, but to the execution, the colouring, or some such other cause.

Imitation, then, is one instinct of our nature. Next, there is the instinct for 'harmony' and rhythm, metres being manifestly sections of rhythm. Persons, therefore, starting with this natural gift developed by degrees their special aptitudes, till their rude improvisations gave birth to Poetry.

Poetry now diverged in two directions, according to the individual character of the writers. The graver spirits imitated noble actions, and the actions of good men. The more trivial sort imitated the actions of meaner persons, at first composing satires, as the former did hymns to the gods and the praises of famous men. A poem of the satirical kind cannot indeed be put down to any author earlier than Homer; though many such writers probably there were. But from Homer onward, instances can be cited, his own Margites, for example, and other similar compositions. The appropriate metre was also here introduced; hence the measure is still called the iambic or lampooning measure, being that in which people lampooned one another. Thus the older poets were distinguished as writers of heroic or of lampooning verse.

As, in the serious style, Homer is pre-eminent among poets, for he alone combined dramatic form with excellence of imitation, so he too first laid down the main lines of Comedy, by dramatising the ludicrous instead of writing personal satire. His Margites bears the same relation to Comedy that the Iliad and Odyssey do to Tragedy. But when Tragedy and Comedy came to light, the two classes of poets still followed their natural bent: the lampooners became writers of Comedy, and the Epic poets were succeeded by Tragedians, since the drama was a larger and higher form of art."

Stretch

1. Return to your companion book.

2. Scan and highlight in green as described in this chapter.

3. Notice how long it takes you to complete a green scan. It should take only a few seconds per page, though it will sometimes take longer than pink, depending on the writer's style.

4. Keep this book nearby for the next exercise.

Nota Bene

Having completed the green scan, you are oriented toward the text you have chosen to read. You know how long it will take you to read it (from scanning with initial questions), you know many of the key words (from scanning with pink), and you know the structure of the text (from scanning with green)—and a great deal more. You are ready to read it like you have never read before.

Notes

Chapter Six
Generating Questions

"And let those that play your clowns speak no more than is set down for them . . . though in the meantime some necessary question of the play be then to be considered."

William Shakespeare
Hamlet

By dividing reading into layers, we have relieved the mind of the burden of remembering heaps of unsorted information all at once. The purpose of reading this way is to enable you to participate in the text, not just engage it academically and, for example, remember names for a quiz. Reading is a complex and difficult activity. This approach makes easier what can be made easier.

Now it is nearly time to read the text directly. If reading this guide has made it seem like quite a burden to get to this point, remember that each scan has only taken a matter of seconds. If you are reading, say, a chapter from Plutarch's *Lives,* you may have spent all of five minutes preparing to read it. Chances are, you could already take a quiz on it and do as well as many students. But that isn't the point.

The point is to enter into the text and participate in a dialogue with the author. For that, you are now ready.

Once you have scanned your text four or more times, your mind is ready to start asking more specific questions. Learning to generate these questions has a profound impact on what you discover and appreciate when you read.

Contemplate

- When deciding to purchase a new home, what questions should you ask after learning the price, size, and location?
- If you are planning a trip or a walk or any sort of journey, what sorts of questions are most helpful?
- What kinds of questions do stories tend to answer?
- What kinds of questions does an instruction guide tend to answer?

- What about an essay?
- After introducing yourself to your neighbors, what questions could you ask to learn more about them?
- Do you find it easier to listen to a person about whom you have questions or about whom you have no questions?

Consider

When my neighbor Robin and I learned that another neighbor was moving away, we wondered how long it would be before the new family moved in, how many children they would have, and their ages. Over the years and after welcoming a few neighbors, sometimes we prayed that a family would have children with similar ages, but other times we prayed for neighbors with similar passions. Our first response was like the initial scan when reading a book.

Later, once these new neighbors had moved in, we would glance over our calendars, looking for a time to stop by, welcome them, and invite them over. This calendar scan is much like a quick scan when reading a book.

Finally, we met the neighbors! They were people like us who needed to turn food, water, and shelter into feasts, nourishment, and home. So, we asked questions to introduce ourselves. "What's your name, where are you from, and how long did you live there?" are pink questions, providing us with information about the characters and setting.

Green questions are quite a bit more personal. After all, green is about relationships. We might ask about their schedules, places they go, and even how they set up their yard and household. These questions give us a sense of this family's shape.

After we introduced ourselves to our neighbors and returned home, I thought of more questions. When our new neighbors were relocated from New York, I wanted to ask more questions about their journey to Texas. When Mr. and Mrs. Lutz moved in, I wanted to know more about his World War II experiences.

Did you notice the epigram at the beginning of this guide? Treat books like people and you will make some good friends. We cannot meet a person and then immediately ask him to divulge his greatest sorrows or triumphs. We cannot expect to nurture a friendship with only occasional conversations that we partially listen to. Books are a lot like friends that way.

When we meet new people, we learn about them in layers through multiple interactions—by the mailbox, at the library, in my home, and so forth. When I read a book, I gather information in layers as well. Each scan is really a purposeful time to ask particular questions in an orderly way.

As you transition from scanning to reading, you focus on a few questions that will help you experience the book. These questions should come from your own curiosity, your purposes, and the kind of book you are reading. To help, we have included a brief discussion on the kinds of questions you can ask, though they are virtually unlimited.

There are different sorts of questions, but the best are those you learn to ask by reading with an open spirit that helps you listen to what the book is saying. At this point, you should not be asking questions related to your feelings toward a book, but about the book itself and what it is trying to say.

Although reading a book can feel like a one-sided conversation, with the book doing all of the talking, it becomes two-way when we ask questions about the characters, setting, plot, or problems. The answers to these questions are contained in the text, and pursuing these answers makes us better readers and therefore better able to enjoy good books.

A question that reveals the heart of a story to us could be called a rhetorical or a normative question. Stories are about people who make decisions and act on them. Authors put actors in difficult situations so we can watch how they respond. Do they act wisely, virtuously, and effectively?

The question behind every story is, "What should he do?" Or, in the past tense, "Should he have done that?"

After scanning your book, write down a few questions to answer while you read (three to five is about right). Questions are our guides on the journey with a book. To read with a question in mind is to read with purpose. Interestingly, it is also true that if I look for one thing, I will notice many more things.

Suppose you are going to read the *Odyssey*. After scanning, you might ask questions like, "Where does Odysseus go on his journey home? What troubles does he encounter? Should he stop at any point along the way?" Or you might ask, "Should Penelope wait for him?"

For *The Great Gatsby*, you might ask, "What kind of car does Gatsby drive and why? Why does the narrator refer to the billboard with the eyes so often? What exactly is Gatsby trying to prove?"

Make up your own questions! As you can see from the range of questions above, you can and should ask from a very wide range of angles. You will probably find it easiest to start with simpler and more concrete questions and work your way up to more abstract questions.

Here are some examples that might help you get started.

Examples of literary questions

- How does the setting or location influence the story?
- How is character X like and different from character Y?
- What problem does the main character(s) wrestle with?
- What previous actions or events complicate the problem?
- What will he decide?
- What will affect this decision?
- What are the results of his decision?
- What literary devices does the author use?
- What themes does the author develop and how does he embody them?
- What motifs flow through the book?
- How much of the backstory do we learn and what is it?
- Compare any two characters, settings, or actions (or anything else).

Examples of rhetorical or normative questions

- Should character X have done Z?
- What should X do?
- Was his decision wise?
- Is he acting honorably?
- Is this cause noble?
- Is this war just?
- Is this action consistent with the character's beliefs?

Advanced philosophical/theological questions

- What does this tell me about mankind?
- What does this tell me about creation?
- What does this tell me about God?
- In light of this, how should I live or what should I do?

Compare

- How is asking a book questions like asking questions of another person?
- How are they different?
- How does asking a book questions affect the way you read it?
- How do these decisions differ from one another?

Generating Questions

1. Think of 3 to 5 questions to ask about the section you are reading.
2. Write them somewhere convenient, such as in the front of your book, in the front of each chapter, or in a notebook
3. Read the section and search for answers to your questions.

Describe

Describe in your own words how to generate questions.

Practice

1. Flip back through this guide. Remind yourself of what you have seen.

2. Decide on one to five questions to guide you as you read the remaining chapter of this book. For example, what skill is this chapter sharing (nature), what is its purpose, and how do I treat this skill appropriately (propriety)?

3. Turn to Chapter Five in this guide.

4. Decide on one to five questions to guide you. Write them in the notes section at the end of this chapter.

Stretch

1. Return to your companion book.

2. Generate three to five questions.

3. Write them in the front of the book or somewhere convenient.

4. Keep your companion book nearby for the next exercise.

Nota Bene

Sometimes one or all of your questions can be asked of each chapter. In these instances, write a prompt on the first or last page of each chapter and spend time at the end of the chapter writing your answers. Answering the question in writing is a blessing.

For example, when reading Shakespeare's Hamlet, *each scene could have two companion questions: What is the issue here and who is the most persuasive concerning it?*

When reading Homer's Odyssey, *each book could have three companion questions: what is the problem, what decision is made, and what is the aftermath?*

While reading Dante's Inferno, each canto could have three companion questions: Where are they (place), what kind of people are there (purpose), and does the punishment match the sin (moral).

Notes

Part Two
Reading

Chapter Seven
Yellow Read

....

"But in the meantime, you must be content, I say, to be misunderstood for a while. We are all very anxious to be understood, and it is very hard not to be. But there is one thing much more necessary."

"What is that, grandmother?"

"To understand other people."

George MacDonald
The Princess and the Goblin

It is time to read! Having scanned multiple times and asked guiding questions, now you are ready to read in a more focused way than ever before.

The next three chapters describe how and why to highlight in yellow, blue, and orange. After you've read and practiced all three chapters, you will read with all three colors at hand (you won't have to read three times!). But first, to practice, just learn yellow.

You use the yellow highlighter to note the flow of thought. In narrative, that means main actors and main actions. In an exposition, it means main subjects and their predicates (what is being said about the subjects).

Contemplate

- When you watch the news, do you expect them to show a complete video of an entire event or game? How do they decide what to include?
- If you wanted to quickly "catch someone up" with a story so he could continue listening or watching from the middle, what information would you share?
- If you bring your car to the mechanic, do you want him to give you a detailed description of how something went wrong with your car and how he is going to fix it? What do you want to know?
- What is a subject and what is a predicate?
- If a child starts telling you a story, do you want him to include everything that comes to his mind? What do you want to hear?

Consider

What is the last story you read? Have you encouraged any friends to read it too? Sharing stories gives us joy. Sometimes the story is long, like the *Odyssey*, but other times it is short, like "Frog and Toad Are Friends: The Garden." Since both of these stories are beautiful, I want my children and friends to know them. I could read aloud Homer's words to tell Odysseus' story, but usually summarizing the story is most helpful and realistic.

What do we include when we retell a story? If we are good story-tellers, we do not get lost in all the details. We don't say everything we know about the setting or the minor characters. Unless something else was uniquely important, we share who was doing what. Toad tended his garden. Frog admired the garden. Toad gave Frog some seeds. Frog planted the seeds. Frog sang, read, and shouted at them. Each of these sentences focuses on who was doing what to keep the main action of the story advancing.

When we read a story, our minds need to keep track of the characters and their actions.

Highlighting in yellow helps us summarize the story by focusing our attention on the main flow of thought. It helps us track the main actors precisely because their actions make up that flow of thought.

If we are reading an expository or technical text, the flow of thought usually revolves around an idea rather than a character. In that case, treat that idea like a character. Ask what is being said about it, and distinguish details from main ideas.

Sometimes, you will already have highlighted the characters

or ideas with pink. If so, don't highlight over them, because it will turn orange. Note what is said about the actor or idea and highlight it in yellow if it is a main idea. Do not highlight prepositional phrases or subordinate clauses unless absolutely necessary.

Yellow highlighting provides continual practice in what has come to be called critical thinking. It does take practice, because you have to make decisions about how important an idea is to the text. This is why it can be so valuable for children. They must read, not to skim information for a quiz, but to make judgements about how important an idea is in the overall story or argument. It would be hard to exaggerate the importance of this skill in coaching good readers.

On the other hand, because it requires critical thinking, logic, and judgment, the best way to learn how to highlight with yellow is simply to practice.

It's not as hard as it might sound on paper, but it does take younger children many years and lots of practice to learn it.

Compare

- How is watching the news like highlighting in yellow?
- How is listening to a story told by a friend like highlighting in yellow?
- Compare yellow highlighting with pink and green. How are they similar? How are they different?
- How does highlighting in yellow affect the way you read?

Describe

Describe in your own words how to read and highlight with yellow.

Reading with Yellow

1. Who is the main actor in the paragraph or section? Highlight it with yellow.
2. What is the main thing he does or experiences? Highlight it or a key word or phrase that captures it with yellow.
3. With non-narrative, what is the main idea (subject) and the main thing said about it (predicate)? Highlight it with yellow (unless it is already pink).
4. When you highlight with yellow, less is often more. If you highlight more than you need, it won't be "highlighted" any more!

Practice

1. Turn to Chapter Five in this guide. You used pink highlights to reveal characters and green highlights to reveal structure.

2. Read the texts with a yellow highlighter in hand and highlight with yellow as described in this chapter.

Stretch

1. Return to your companion book.

2. In the selected chapter, read and highlight in yellow the main characters and their main actions. Some characters' names will

already be pink; this is expected. Add the yellow to their main actions, but avoid highlighting details that are less essential to the story.

3. If the text is expository or technical rather than narrative, highlight the main subject and main predicate in each paragraph.

4. Keep your companion book nearby for the next exercise.

<u>Nota Bene</u>

This chapter and the next two chapters present three colors keyed to three sets of questions: yellow, blue, and orange.

Remember, attentive reading has three stages: scanning, reading, and reviewing. When we scan, we scan each chapter or section for one reason at a time.

In a similar way, highlighting enables us to read without dividing our attention between the different sorts of questions that our minds ask and the books answer.

Nevertheless, as you will see, you can have all three highlighters handy while you read. You need only read the text one time rather than three (which is often not possible). For now, give your attention to yellow highlighting.

Notes

Chapter Eight
Blue Read

....

"[R]ight about the hollow cavern extended a flourishing growth of vine that ripened with grape clusters. Next to it there were four fountains, and in each of them ran shining water, each next to each, but turned to run in sundry directions; and round about there were meadows growing soft with parsley and violets, and even a god who came into that place would have admired what he saw, the heart delighted within him."

Homer's *Odyssey*

Blue highlighting introduces a new emphasis. By now you have studied the text as much as most people ever will, though in a much more efficient way than most people do. As you master these tools, the pleasure of reading with them will only increase.

But blue is very personal. In essence, if you particularly like the way the author said something, highlight it in blue.

There seem to be three main reasons for highlighting in blue. First, like the quotation from Homer above, a text is memorable. Second, like the scene described in that passage, it is admirable. And third, it causes the heart to delight. If something is memorable, admirable, or delightful, highlight it in blue.

Contemplate

- Do you, your children, or your friends ever quote lines from movies or songs? What about passages from literature or the Bible?
- Why do people find some lines memorable and not others?
- When you hear lines recited, does the discussion often bring out responses from other parts of the movie or literature?
- Do you ever find yourself wanting to remember a line or passage from something you are reading? What do you do when that happens?
- What makes you want to remember or return to these lines?

Consider

Special occasions in a family draw out our desire to remember. We take a multitude of photographs and we collect mementoes. A belt from Philmont Scout Ranch, a rock from a diving trip, a bride's wedding dress, a lock of hair from a baby's first hair cut, a college ring or graduation tassel, a much-loved baseball glove, license plates from old cars, or our grandfather's hand tools—all of these are keepsakes that bring us joy when we use, recall, and remember the stories surrounding them.

When I look at photographs from a fishing vacation, I can see the rods, reels, and smiles, but I also remember meeting the dear man who carried my children on his back across the rising river. I also remember standing around the tailgate of our truck, eating delicious foods, and sharing them with this surprised man.

Keepsakes and pictures recall whole stories and events of which they have become symbols—vessels that we use to carry the experiences in our souls.

Reading is like that too. Sometimes we simply want to remember what we are reading. Maybe it offers us wisdom we do not want to forget, or it expresses something in a way we admire, or it delights our hearts the way the quotation does from Homer at the beginning of this chapter.

Highlight these passages in blue!

Because they are so personal, blue highlights vary for each reader. For example, my son and I (Andrea) read *Mere Christianity* by C. S. Lewis this year. It has been great fun to share blues and to see passages that one of us highlighted but the other did not and also passages that we both highlighted.

He highlighted, "If somebody else made me, for his own purposes, then I shall have a lot of duties which I should not have if I simply belonged to myself." In Lewis' previous paragraph I highlighted, "You cannot make men good by law: and without good men you cannot have a good society." We both enjoyed Lewis' sculptor shop image: "This world is a great sculptor's shop. We are the statues and there is a rumor going round the shop that some of us are some day going to come to life."

As you can see, blue is the most personal of colors—it reflects your response to the text. You highlight in blue because you liked what you read. You need no other justification. While reading *Watership Down* by Richard Adams, I highlighted in blue, "A spirit of happy mischief entered into Hazel." My heart also delighted when I read Blackberry's words, "'We've all got to stop running one day, you know." But who knows, maybe those words mean nothing to you. That's okay. It's *my* book.

Interestingly, the fact that blue is so personal can lead to wonderful group discussions about the text. I (Andrew) frequently begin a discussion about, say, a book in the *Iliad*, by asking students to "share their blues." Going page by page turns the blue sharing into a very pleasant and interesting review of the section my students have just read. It also gives an additional, personal motivation to read it beyond academic performance. It shows them that I care about what they think and feel.

If you find something memorable, admirable, or delightful, highlight it in blue!

A technical note: blue and yellow combine to make green, so if you like a passage a lot, be sure to highlight it in blue before you turn it yellow. If it is already yellow, just put a blue mark in the margin. If it is already blue and you want to make it yellow, put a yellow mark in the margin.

Compare

- What do taking pictures, saving mementos, and reading a book have in common?
- How is highlighting in blue like highlighting in yellow? How is it different? How does it compare to pink and green?
- What questions do you ask for each color?
- How does highlighting in blue affect the way you approach a text?
- What can you do more easily with a text once you have highlighted passages in blue?

Reading with Blue

1. Read with your blue highligher at hand.
2. When you read something memorable, admirable, or delightful (i.e., something you particularly like), highlight in blue.

Describe:

Describe in your own words how and why to highlight in blue.

Practice

1. Turn to the practice texts you have highlighted in pink, green, and yellow in Chapter Five.

2. Read them again, this time with a blue highlighter in hand.

3. If you read anything particularly memorable, admirable, or delightful, highlight it in blue.

Stretch

1. Pick up your companion book.

2. As you read, highlight in blue the passages that are particularly memorable, admirable, or delightful.

3. Keep your companion book nearby for the next exercise.

<u>Nota Bene</u>

The reason you highlight in blue while also highlighting in yellow is that the combination reflects the way the mind behaves. You can be reading along, flowing with the thought stream, when suddenly the flow hits a rock or a bend that makes the light leap from the page. You are jolted by its beauty and want to stop and notice it. Do! Highlight it in blue.

Notes

Chapter Nine
Orange Read

....

"As when a donkey, stubborn and hard to move, goes
into a cornfield in despite of boys, and many sticks
have been broken upon him, but he gets in and goes on
eating the deep grain, and the children beat him with
sticks, but their strength is infantile; yet at last by hard
work they drive him out when he is glutted with eating;
so the high-hearted Trojans and companions in arms
gathered from far places kept after great Aias, the son
of Telamon, stabbing always with their spears at the
centre of the great shield."

Homer's *Iliad*

The hardest thing about explaining how to highlight with orange is that it is your color to do with as you wish. It's a miscellaneous color, used to highlight things you haven't already highlighted in another color but that you think should still be highlighted. We'll give you some ideas below. For example, I (Andrew) like to use it to highlight literary devices, like the epic simile you see above from Homer's *Iliad*. But you should feel complete freedom to use it for anything you want to highlight.

Contemplate

- Does your kitchen or workshop have a junk drawer?
- If you keep files or a budget, do you keep a miscellaneous category?
- Can you think of anything you might want to highlight that has not already been covered?

Consider

Orange is a gift. You can adapt it to whatever you determine you (or your students) need to notice. Really, you choose. You can even use it differently from book to book.

When I (Andrew again) first started highlighting, I found things I was not sure I agreed with and wanted to come back to later so I could take them up with the author. I would highlight them in orange. When I was teaching Homer, I discovered that he wrote a lot of magnificent epic similes. I wanted to find them easily, so I highlighted them in orange.

You might highlight things you are learning or teaching about reading, writing, even logic or rhetoric (i.e., about thinking). For example, you might identify cause and effect relationships, literary devices (metaphors, personification, etc.), or the premises and conclusion of an argument. Or you might follow a theme, such as honor or memory, or a motif, such as animals or plants. Students could be instructed to mark appeals to ethos, pathos, and logos. They could use orange to identify when a change occurs in a character.

If you or your students are learning classical rhetoric, such as *The Lost Tools of Writing*, you could instruct them to highlight schemes and tropes in orange. When they do, they fill a treasure chest with beautiful artifacts that can serve as types or models. What else might you want them to notice?

If there is something you want to note or teach your students to note and it is not yet highlighted in another color, highlight it in orange!

<u>Compare</u>

- How is keeping a junk drawer like highlighting in orange? How are they different?
- How is highlighting in orange like pink, green, yellow, and blue? How is it different?
- How does having the orange highlighter available affect the way you approach a text?

<u>Describe</u>

- Describe reading with orange in your own words.
- What sorts of thing might you want to highlight in orange?

Reading with Orange

1. What do you want to note when you read? (or what do you want your students to note when they read?)
2. Search for it and use orange to highlight in when you find it.
3. Remember, orange adapts to the needs of the reader.
4. It is the least important color, so you should not feel compelled to use it if you do not have a reason for it.

Practice

1. Turn to Chapter Five.

2. Select a reason to use orange (e.g., literary device, theme, things you disagree with, etc.)

3. Read Chapter Five again with an orange highlighter in hand and a purpose in mind. Remember, orange is a gift. If you do not know how to start, try one of the ideas mentioned above, such as schemes and tropes (literary devices).

Stretch

1. Return to your companion book.

2. Select a reason to use orange.

3. Read and highlight the chosen section in orange.

4. Keep your companion book nearby for the next exercise.

Nota Bene

You now know how to use all five highlighters, two for scanning and three for reading. Remember that each highlighter is used to note answers to a different kind of question. It started very precisely and simply with pink. By the time you read with orange, you are exercising much more judgment about your markings.

It is important to scan in layers, but to read with all three reading highlighters at once. You may find yourself following the flow of thought, being interrupted by a beautiful and memorable expression, and noticing a theme or device that you are looking for, all in rapid succession. When you have the highlighters near at hand, it is easy to mark them and either stop and reflect or continue, whichever is more fitting under the circumstances.

Of course, like any skill, this takes practice. But what you are practicing is one of the most important skills you can learn: close reading. It is worth every second.

Notes

Part Three
Review

Chapter Ten
What Review Is

"Man's real work is to look at the things of the world and to love them for what they are. That is, after all, what God does, and man was not made in God's image for nothing. The fruits of attention can be seen in all the arts, crafts, and sciences. It can cost him time and effort, but it pays handsomely. ...[H]is inattention costs him dearly. ...[E]very time he regards not what a thing is but what it can be made to mean to him ... he is left with ... an idol."

Robert Farrar Capon
The Supper of the Lamb

You have scanned, questioned, and read your companion book, following the exercises outlined in the previous chapters. No doubt, you have read more closely than during a normal reading activity and maybe more closely than you ever have before.

Now it is time to apply the lacquer: to establish your hold over what is yours, to make it more a part of yourself.

The third stage in this reading guide can be summed up in the word "review," though we think what you will actually do is much more interesting than that word might make it feel, especially if you like the book you are reading.

Review consists of four actions:

- *Narrate*
- *Answer*
- *Discuss*
- *Record*

Narrate

The first step to secure what you have read is to recite or narrate it to someone else. Narrating is straight forward: Find someone you can convince to listen to you while you talk about the book.

Narrating does not require memorizing the text, but telling it in your own words. If the text was long, you should summarize it. If it is short, a paraphrase will be fine. If you find you do remember the text word for word, you can recite it, but do not let the repetition keep you from thinking about it. If you would like more ideas on reciting or narrating, Charlotte Mason and her followers are the best source of which we are aware.

Having scanned and read the text, you might surprise yourself by how much you remember. However, if you struggle (and we all do, especially at first) use the structure tips you learned while highlighting in green. If the text is narrative, move from scene to scene with the actors and note what they do or what they see in each place as they come and go. If it is expository, treat the ideas like actors and the questions like scenes. Follow them as they move from question to question. Pay special attention to illustrations because you will find them much easier to remember.

If you are reading a book with untitled sections, you may find it helpful to come up with brief phrases or even single words to give a title to each section. At first, you will find it easiest to copy a phrase from the author that seems to label the whole section. In time, come up with your own words to summarize the section in a single phrase. For example, we named the section you are reading "Narrate." Can you come up with another title?

Narrations, titles, and summaries like those described above are excellent tools to help us remember what we have read and to prepare for insightful discussions.

Answer

Once you narrate the text, return to the questions you wrote after you scanned but before you read your section. Answer them, either aloud or on paper. If you do not know the answers, either give yourself some time to think about them or return to the text and find the answer there. Then review the questions an hour or so later to remind yourself.

One advantage you will enjoy when you highlight is that those

CiRCE GUIDE TO READING

answers are usually pretty easy to find.

Discuss

This guide is not about book discussions, but right now it wishes it was. There can be little doubt that the most significant way to improve your reading is to prepare for and participate in a group discussion. All of us need to hear what other people get from a book that we do not. And preparing helps us focus our attention when we read.

Everything you have done so far in this guide has prepared you to discuss your text confidently. Simply sharing blues can lead to amazing shared experiences. Add to that a memory full of new settings and characters, an awareness of the story's structure, and attunement to the flow of thought and you have a set of tools that has prepared you thoroughly for a common experience with the text. We hope that the fruit you produce is a deeper appreciation for great books and the wisdom and joy they give you, not only in yourself, but in those with whom you share the experience.

Record

You will also want to record your favorite passages in a commonplace book, which is a way of collecting your blues and insights and recording them in a separate notebook or journal set aside for that purpose.

Now I (Andrew), being a man, am perfectly happy to grab the nearest notebook or scrap of paper and scribble a quotation on it, but the other I (Andrea) being a lady, takes a much more civilized approach.

The next chapter goes into some detail about how to build a great commonplace book. But if all of that is too time consuming, just grab the nearest notebook and play the man!

Notes

Chapter Eleven
Commonplacing

....

*"All that happened since Bilbo left the Shire was passing
through his mind, and he recalled and pondered everything that he could remember of Gandalf's words."*

J.R.R. Tolkien
The Lord of the Rings

A commonplace book is a crown or a garland for a close read. It is where you keep a permanent record in your own hand of your favorite passages and it is where you return to gather inspiration and wisdom for the journey ahead. You might think of it as your own portable Rivendell.

Contemplate

- Have you ever written something down just so you could come back and think about it later?
- Where do you keep information or ideas that you want to remember?

Consider

In our home (Andrea's) we collect the same sorts of things in a few places set aside for them. Near the front door on a thin blue table a small silver bowl collects keys when we return home. Just beyond the table is an antique, free-standing coat rack that gathers jackets, hats, and bags. An open shelf below the small silver bowl holds a basket filled with cheap flashlights. The flashlights provide inexpensive fun for the kids and their friends, enabling them to explore outside after dark while the grown-ups continue their conversations. Our family and friends know these common places to find or put away these common items.

We want a record of what we read, and keeping a common place to collect quotations is a beloved way that many people employ to keep such a record.

One way to think about commonplaces is to see them as topics that we share (i.e., have in common with each other), such as fear, love, hope, freedom, honor, home, order, friendship, and faith.

Having highlighted in blue, you now have a store of unsorted quotations. In your commonplace book, you can categorize those quotations and look them up when you want to think about that subject.

How do we start a commonplace book? First, consider the materials. What we are doing and the materials we are using need to be in harmony with one another. The commonplace book itself ought to be lasting and beautiful since we are recording words that should endure. It should be a book that comfortably fits in size with the other books we are reading and is easy to carry. The pens we use should smoothly flow across the paper since we should also enjoy the writing experience. Black and blue ink do not fade.

Next, consider the structure you will apply to your commonplace. Once you establish the form, you can fill it. Begin with a title page. Commonplace books are personal and deserve your name written on the first page. Reserve the next three to four pages for a table of contents that you will update as you add passages. Write page numbers in the same place on each page. An index can be reserved for the final four or more pages if you want to search within your book by category.

Lastly, fill the commonplace book. Using your best handwriting, copy memorable, admirable, and delightful passages from the books you have read. Some of my students alternate their entries in blue and black ink to add visual separation. Writing each entry with a similar pattern can add another layer of beauty to this collection as well.

Here are some possible details to include with a passage: the speaker (when appropriate), author, book title, page number, and ideas captured in that passage. Include the page number

CiRCE GUIDE TO READING

for easy reference.

Here are three ways you can enter passages into a common-place book. Do not let these limit you.

1. Enter passages in categories: This is what we have been describing above. You could separate your commonplace book into sections for passages on man, God, and nature or on faith, hope, and love or any other groups of ideas you are attending to. You could also establish separate sections for quotes, vocabulary words, resources, notes, and memory. This back section of your commonplace book could be a place for entering poems and psalms that you are memorizing.

2. Enter passages from one book at a time: If you enter all the "blues" from one book at a time (e.g., all of your blues from the *Iliad*), then you can also add a larger scripted title of the book on the first page of the section set aside for it. Titles of books can be added to the table of contents in the same order that passages are added to the commonplace book. You could leave a blank page between books.

3. Enter passages from any book in any order: Some people prefer a more random approach to collecting quotations and being inspired. If you are copying "blues" from multiple books at once, then be sure to include the author, title, and page number with each added passage. The table of contents could include each book with a list of page numbers where a passage can be found from that book.

When I pause to enter the last passages from a book into my commonplace, it is as if all the characters and the author are seated around a table with me drinking tea. This ordinary meal, tea among friends, is to be savored. It is a time of synthesizing the ideas in the books in a way that nurtures wisdom and virtue.

Once we have experienced the whole story and are reviewing the passages that brought delight to our souls, we might have a fresh glimpse into the author's idea and the story's power in a light we could not have seen any other way.

Whichever approach you choose for a commonplace book, let it grow like a council of wise men and women who are there to teach and inspire you. The more you receive their counsel, the more you will grow within yourself.

Compare

- How is keeping a commonplace book like gathering objects around the house? How is it different?
- How is commonplacing like highlighting? How is it different?
- How will keeping a commonplace book affect your reading? How is keeping a commonplace book like a meeting of very wise people? Different?
- What advantages do each of the modes of commonplacing offer? What disadvantages? Which do you prefer?

Describe

Describe in your own words how to keep a commonplace book.

Practice

1. Turn to Chapter Five.

2. Did you highlight any passages with blue?

3. Do you want to record any of them for permanent reference or inspiration? Write them in your commonplace book.

4. Purchase, prepare, and fill a commonplace book. Do not worry about messing up; this book is to serve you! You will learn what you need and like by doing it.

Commonplacing

1. After reading and reviewing a section of a text (book, article, people, etc.), flip back through it and read the blues.
2. Are any of these passages so memorable, admirable, and delightful that you want to record them in your commonplace book?
3. Are there categories or common topics they can be sorted under?
4. Hand write those passages into your commonplace book. Include page numbers and update your table of contents.

Stretch

1. Return to your companion book.

2. Did you mark any passages with blue?

3. Do you want to see them on a poster? Are you aching to share that passage with a friend? Do you want to keep any for

permanent reference or inspiration? Copy it into your common-place book.

4. Keep this guidebook and your commonplace book nearby when you read. Use the guidebook as needed; use a commonplace book as much as you can.

Notes

Epilogue

Many of us learned to read like students whose only goal was to score well on a test or a quiz: seeking answers to specified questions, gathering information because someone else told us to, and collecting facts with a supervisor looking over our shoulders making sure we drew the right conclusion.

Reading that way can build a barrier between the reader and his book. He worries more about getting the right answer than hearing the author speak and he develops habits that obscure rather than lead to profound and insightful encounters.

The tools you have learned through this reading guide turn reading into a conversation between the reader and the book, and they prepare you to carry on that conversation with other readers.

We admit that the skills learned will help students perform better on tests and in academic settings (probably exponentially), but that is not why the skills are worth learning.

This guide applies an old-fashioned virtue called love. We believe these tools will help their users love reading, in part because they discipline and equip the reader to read more purposefully and perceptively. More importantly, we believe that helping a student grow is an act of love. *Most* importantly, we believe that by learning to read better, students (and teachers) will grow in wisdom and love for their neighbors in a post-literate culture where these disciplines are much too rare.

Appendix A
Same Skills, Different Ages

I n his book *Norms and Nobility*, David Hicks compared the challenge of the teacher and the challenge of the learner. He wrote, "It is the challenge of teaching to understand what form advanced concepts ought to take . . . while it is the challenge of learning to discipline the unruly and discursive mind, adjusting its disorderliness through rigorous study to the order of logical processes found outside it in the subject matter."

By nature we read in an ordered manner, asking certain questions prior to other questions. Regardless of age, the skills readers learn in this guide follow the natural sequence which our minds follow when they ask questions. Scanning and reading with different layers of questions is the logical process to which the reader must "discipline the unruly and discursive mind."

Developing listening and thinking skills begins when we are young. The skills themselves and their order remain the same, but their practice and use vary with age. As Hamlet says, "the readiness is all."

Readiness is determined partly by age, partly be experience, and partly by natural talent. The younger the student, the more repetition he needs, the more time it takes to absorb the ideas, and the more concrete he needs instruction to be.

I (Andrew) taught this approach to third graders, but each year it took a few months. Teach one color at a time. The older the students, the more quickly they can understand the color scheme (but they also might resist the approach more in middle and high school). Adults have developed strong opinions and habits about reading, so they might embrace or reject this approach. We hope they will find the skills behind the tools helpful, even if the tools don't impress them.

Appendix B
Margin Notes

W riting notes in the margins of books is not a new idea. During the Middle Ages, when books were perhaps most cherished, it was refined to a magnificent art. Margin notes provide an additional way you can dialogue while you read. The blue or black ink ball point pen typically does not fade off the page nor bleed through the paper.

Use the following symbols to notate your books:

? - If you do not understand something, write a question mark in the margin so you can ask a friend during discussion.

! - Surprise, shift, twist, sudden change

Sh - To notate that a "should" question is here that you may want to think on further. Should the actor have performed that action?

) - Echo, a restatement of the same exact words or ideas

Δ - change in character (comes from Greek letter delta, meaning difference)

∗ - Add stars to important blues that remain blues with subsequent readings. Add a star with each new read.

Add these marks to the margin when you notice the five common topics and the special topics:

D - Definition (or mark as noted above)

Ci - Circumstance

R/c - Relationship cause

R/e - Relationship effect

T - Testimony

Av - Advantages

Dv - Disadvantage

AS - An sit, is it so?

QS - Quid sit, what happened or what is it?

QLS - Quale sit, what kind of thing happened?

You should develop your own code for your own purposes. You may find it helpful to learn an editing code from a grammar handbook or a teacher, but that is not the main purpose of these margin notes.

Appendix C
Re-reading a Highlighted Book

E veryone agrees attentive reading is a skill to practice, but some books you will not re-read while other books you will re-read.

What are the benefits to re-reading a highlighted book three years later?

For one thing, you will see improvement in your own reading. As you practice attentive reading skills, those skills will improve; you will notice different characters, actions, or descriptions. You may disagree with your marks during a subsequent reading. Like a craftsman who built a table and sees its flaws and so improves his next project, readers can notice differences in how they understand a book or use highlighters.

For another thing, you will easily review what you discovered earlier.

Each time you read a book it prepares you for the next time you read it (or any other book for that matter). You will find it easy to follow the flow of thought, locate yourself in the structure, and review earlier questions. You will also find old friends highlighted in blue or orange. Most likely, you will know the work so well, even after a period of time, that your experience will be like meeting an old friend.

When you begin attentively reading, write your name and the date in the front of the book. When you return, this note reminds you when you last traveled in these pages, in this place.

What are the benefits of discussing a highlighted book?

The colors are actually answers to questions which reveal patterns. Cause and effect may clearly connect. When re-reading a highlighted book, echoes might reverberate loudly this time. Add a new margin note to indicate echos and possibly the page number to the first reference. The previously highlighted lines also help us find our way home, to the joys and the sorrows of the story.

How do we re-read a highlighted book?

Overall, re-read with a similar pattern: initial scan, glance over the pinks, glance over the greens, and read with yellow. If yellows were not added in a previous read, add that response. If you read a blue and decide again it is certainly a blue, add a star next to it. You could also write a key word answering why it is a blue; for example, it demonstrates hope, it expresses friendship, it embodies courage. You will notice some things that you did not notice on an earlier read. For example, you may notice that the author defines some key words; highlight the word and underline the definition pink. Sometimes I (Andrea) add an equal sign (=) between the term and the definition.

Some readers worry that they will be distracted by the highlighting when they return to a book. This is possible, even likely for people who are learning to highlight later in life (after junior high school). But, one, you will get used to it and, two, it is worth it.

The habits of inquiry that you develop through this approach will always make you a better reader, even if you do not use the highlighters. But the efficiency the highlighters add to any study or research, and the ease with which you can move around a highlighted text, take your reading from walking on the road to galloping on a horse.

Recommended Resources

Books on Reading Well
- *How to Read Slowly* by James Sire
- *Beauty in the Word* by Stratford Caldecott
- *The ABCs of Reading* by Ezra Pound
- *The Techniques of Reading* by Horace Judson
- *How to Read a Book* by Mortimer Adler
- *The Evelyn Wood Seven-Day Speed Reading and Learning Program* by Stanley D. Frank

Commonplace Books
- Moleskine Classic Plain Notebook or Cashier, 5 x 8.25
- Apica, Rhodia, and Clairefontaine are also good notebooks.
- Leather bound blank book
- Lasting journal with lines, dotted lines, squares, or blank pages

Highlighters
- Sharpie retractable highlighter set
- Major Accent non-fluorescent yellow highlighter (this will not fade)
- Bible highlighter set
- Crayola crayons

Writing Tools
- For colored pens, Stabilo point 88. I (Andrea) use these in black to write in my commonplace book, and the colors are nice for adding illuminations. I have a few point 68 in colors for titles. These will become water colors if "painted" with a wet brush. Can be found in art stores.
- For pencils, Paper Mate Clearpoint 0.5mm mechanical pencil
- For a fountain pen, Lamy Vista Fountain Pen

Miscellaneous
- Post-it Flags for bookmarks that do not fall out